MONTANA

Past and Present

Jason Porterfield

rosen publishing's
rosen central®

New York

Published in 2011 by The Rosen Publishing Group, Inc.
29 East 21st Street, New York, NY 10010

First Edition

Library of Congress Cataloging-in-Publication Data

Porterfield, Jason.
Montana : past and present / Jason Porterfield. — 1st ed.
    p. cm. — (The United States: past and present)
Includes bibliographical references and index.
ISBN 978-1-4358-9486-0 (library binding)
ISBN 978-1-4358-9513-3 (pbk.)
ISBN 978-1-4358-9547-8 (6-pack)
1. Montana—Juvenile literature. I. Title.
F731.3.P67 2011
978.6—dc22

                                                                    2010000415

Manufactured in Malaysia

CPSIA Compliance Information: Batch #S10YA: For further information, contact Rosen Publishing, New York, New York, at 1-800-237-9932.

On the cover: Top left: In 1876, more than two hundred American soldiers were killed at Custer's Last Stand at the Battle of Little Bighorn, one of the last victories for Native Americans fighting for their land. Top right: Montana is the only U.S. state that produces platinum and palladium, two rare metals. Here, an ore sample is tested at a mining plant. Bottom: Montana's Glacier National Park features forests and meadows, lakes and valleys, rugged Rocky Mountain peaks, and remnant glaciers dating from the ice age ten thousand years ago.

Contents

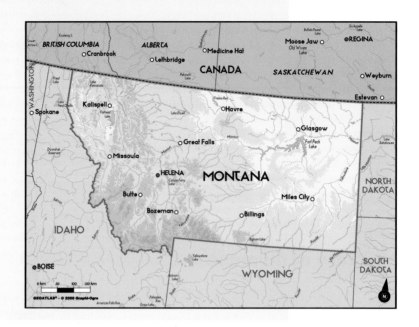

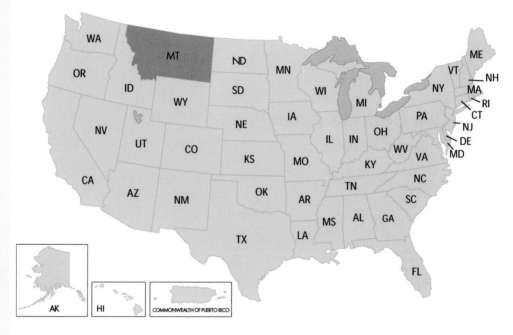

Montana is the only state that borders three different Canadian provinces. The capital city of Helena is also the county seat of Lewis and Clark County.

Introduction

Montana is a vast state defined by the rugged Rocky Mountains, the high plains of the Missouri Plateau, and cascading rivers. Located in the far northwestern United States, Montana is relatively isolated from the more populous regions of the country. Though its size makes it the fourth biggest state, with an area of 147,046 square miles (380,849 square kilometers), it is also one of the least populated. The state's many nicknames, including Big Sky Country and the Treasure State, refer to Montana's natural beauty and plentiful natural resources. The state's name even comes from the Spanish word for mountains.

Montana shares borders with Wyoming to the south, North Dakota and South Dakota to the east, and Idaho to the west. Its northern boundary is marked by an international border with Canada. The Canadian provinces of British Columbia, Alberta, and Saskatchewan all lie to the north, making Montana the only state to share a border with three different provinces.

Though Montana remains off the beaten path for many travelers, millions come to the state for its two famous national parks, Yellowstone National Park and Glacier National Park. Those who visit often return later to discover Montana's rich Native American cultures, abundant wildlife, and mining and ranching legacy. The state continues to attract the adventurous and restless and welcome explorers of all kinds.

Chapter 1

THE GEOGRAPHY OF MONTANA

Montana can be split into two geographic regions. The western-most portion of the state is named for the Rocky Mountains that dominate the landscape. To the east, the Great Plains region covers two-thirds of the state.

The mountains formed when portions of the earth's crust called tectonic plates ground together, forcing massive rocks upward. Later, lava bubbled up to the surface and formed more rock on the new mountains as it cooled and hardened to stone. The glaciers that once covered much of North America carved peaks and valleys into the Rockies. In the northern part of the region, narrow valleys separate the mountains. Farther to the south, the valleys are much broader, with some up to 40 miles (64 km) wide.

Montana is one of six Rocky Mountain states, along with Idaho, Colorado, Wyoming, Utah, and New Mexico. Montana's Rocky Mountain region includes more than fifty different mountain ranges. These ranges include the Cabinet, Crazy, Mission, Tobacco Root, Bridger, Madison, Big Belt, Absaroka, Beartooth, Ruby, Flathead, Beaverhead, Gallatin, Swan, Little Belt, Bitterroot, and Lewis. At 12,807 feet (3,904 meters) tall, Granite Peak in the Beartooth Mountains in the south-central part of the state is the highest peak in Montana and the tenth highest in the nation.

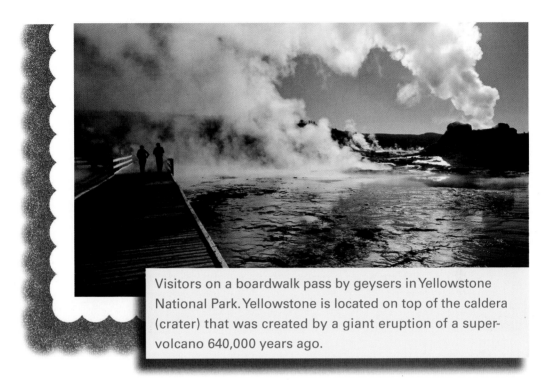

Visitors on a boardwalk pass by geysers in Yellowstone National Park. Yellowstone is located on top of the caldera (crater) that was created by a giant eruption of a super-volcano 640,000 years ago.

The state's two national parks, Yellowstone National Park and Glacier National Park, are located in the Rockies. Glacier National Park is part of the Waterton-Glacier International Peace Park, which is located in both Montana and Canada. The park was established in 1910 and contains more than 1,000,000 acres (404,685 hectares) and includes two mountain ranges, more than three hundred lakes, a mix of dense forests and alpine tundra, and twenty-seven glaciers.

Yellowstone National Park is located in the southwestern portion of the state, near Virginia City. Yellowstone was established in 1903 and was the first national park in the country. Most of the park is located in Wyoming, but Montana's portion includes plentiful wild-life and geological features such as geysers, mud pots, and steam vents called fumaroles. Montana's Absaroka-Beartooth Wilderness is located along the park's northern border and includes two national

A fence runs along the edge of a field on a Montana ranch. The Great Plains region is known for its open grasslands punctuated by scenic mountains.

forests, one thousand lakes, and twenty-eight mountain peaks higher than 12,000 feet (3,657 m).

Most of Montana's Great Plains region—sometimes called the Missouri Plateau—is flat or made up of low hills, broken occasionally by isolated mountains. Streams and rivers cut low valleys into the plains. The elevation in the Great Plains ranges from 2,000 feet (610 m) to 3,300 feet (1,000 m). The region is marked by badlands, mesas, buttes, gullies, and canyons.

The Great Plains region is divided into two areas. The northern plains were once covered with glaciers and are marked by lakes and rugged terrain. The southern section is drier and smoother, consisting mostly of open grassland. In the southeastern corner of the state is a dry and heavily eroded region called the Badlands. Over millions of years, water and wind sculpted the region into steep hills, ditches, and canyons. Many of the exposed rocks were shaped into unusual formations.

Lakes and Waterways

Part of the Continental Divide runs along the Rockies in Montana. Also called the Great Divide, it determines the direction that rivers and streams flow. Rivers east of

A freeway passes over the headwaters of the Missouri River. Lewis and Clark's expedition reached the Missouri River headwaters in the summer of 1805.

the Continental Divide drain into the Atlantic Ocean, and rivers west of the Continental Divide drain into the Pacific Ocean. Montana's river systems also drain north into the Arctic Ocean through the Hudson Bay. It is the only state with rivers that drain in three different directions and into three separate oceans.

The Missouri River and the Yellowstone River are the two most important rivers in the state. The Missouri River forms in southwestern Montana, whereas the Gallatin, Jefferson, and Madison rivers flow down from the Rockies and meet. From that point, the Missouri

Glacier National Park

Glacier National Park is often considered the centerpiece of a network of Rocky Mountain parks called the Crown of the Continent Ecosystem, a largely untouched region that covers about 1,600 square miles (4,140 sq km). During the late nineteenth century, much of the eastern half of the park was spared from logging and mining as part of the Blackfoot reservation. The Blackfoot tribe sold about 800,000 acres (323,748 ha) of the land to the U.S. government in 1895 for $1.5 million, and it became a forest preserve in 1897 before becoming a national park in 1910. In 1932, the park combined with Waterton Lakes National Park in Canada to form Waterton-Glacier International Peace Park in honor of the close ties between the United States and Canada.

After the park was established and visitors began relying more on automobiles, the National Park Service began work on the Going-to-the-Sun Road in 1917. Completed in 1932, the 53-mile-long (85 km) road was named for Going-to-the-Sun Mountain, a peak that dominates the eastbound view from Logan Pass. The narrow, twisting route is the only road that crosses through the park.

Today, the park receives millions of visitors every year, with many coming to see the glaciers for which the park is named. These glaciers are the remnants of the massive glaciers that carved mountains, shaped valleys, and later melted to form lakes along the Rockies. The largest of these glaciers is Grinnell Glacier.

However, the glaciers are steadily melting due to warmer temperatures and fewer snowstorms to replenish them, a trend seen in nonpolar ice around the world. When the park was first explored and surveyed in the late nineteenth century, there were about 150 glaciers in the region. In recent years, that number has been reduced to twenty-seven with the remaining glaciers continuing to shrink. Scientists watching the glaciers predict that if current global warming trends continue, all of the park's glaciers could disappear in the coming decades.

flows east for 2,315 miles (3,725 km) to the Mississippi River. Other Montana rivers flowing into the Missouri include the Sun, Milk, Teton, Poplar, Judith, and Marias rivers. During the nineteenth century, the Missouri served as a gateway for pioneers coming into Montana.

The Yellowstone River begins in Wyoming and flows east and north from Yellowstone National Park before joining with the Missouri. The Yellowstone River is the chief tributary of the Missouri and the longest river without a dam in the continental United States. Rivers that flow into the Yellowstone include the Boulder, Bighorn, and Powder rivers.

Hundreds of natural and man-made lakes dot Montana's terrain. Flathead Lake is located in northwestern Montana and is the largest natural lake in the state. It covers about 195 square miles (505 sq km) and is the largest freshwater lake west of the Mississippi River and one of the three hundred largest freshwater lakes in the world. The largest man-made lake in the state is Fort Peck Lake on the Missouri River, at 383 square miles (992 sq km).

Climate

Montana's weather can vary widely due to the state's vast size and differences in elevation. West of the Continental Divide, the climate is affected by winds from the Pacific Ocean. Summers in the west are cooler and winters warmer. Summer temperatures in the west range from 79 to 85 degrees Fahrenheit (26 to 29 degrees Celsius), and winter temperatures average 20°F (-7°C). In the east, summer temperatures average 89°F (32°C), and winter temperatures average 14°F (-10°C).

Winters in the east are usually long and harsh and characterized by blizzards. Sometimes warm, dry winds, called chinooks, blow down from the mountains and onto the eastern plains during the winter. These winds can quickly melt snowdrifts and raise temperatures around the state.

Precipitation also varies between the east and the west. The western slopes of the Rockies usually get more than 32 inches (81 centimeters) of precipitation each year. The drier eastern slopes and plains get only about 13 inches (33 cm) per year.

Plants and Animals

More than two thousand species of wildflower grow throughout Montana, including lupine, sweet clover, goldenrod, shooting stars, aster, and violet. The few fruits native to Montana grow in the river valleys. These fruits include chokecherry, buffalo berry, and service-berry.

Montana's mostly treeless plains are covered with grasses such as buffalo grass and blue grama grass. Desert plants, like cacti, and shrubs, like sagebrush, grow in drier areas. Trees such as willow, cottonwood, and poplar grow in the river valleys and upland regions. The western mountains are home to forests of coniferous trees such as ponderosa pine, lodgepole pine, Douglas fir, larch, juniper, spruce, and red cedar.

Montana has a wide variety of wildlife. Deer, pronghorns, black-footed ferrets, and burrowing owls live on the prairie, as do prairie dogs, which inhabit networks of holes and tunnels. Animals found in the Rocky Mountains include grizzly bears and black bears, moose, elk, pronghorns, golden eagles, mountain goats, bighorn sheep, mule deer, and wolves. Smaller animals include otters, coyotes, beavers, pumas, bobcats, lynx, minks, weasels, and pikas. Bison, once

The gray wolf, a native species of Montana, went extinct in the state by the 1930s due to hunting. Reintroduced to the region in the 1980s, the wolf population has begun to make a recovery.

common throughout the state, are now found only in a few protected areas, like the National Buffalo Range in Flathead Valley.

About 380 species of birds are found in Montana. Wild geese, ducks, and whooping cranes spend their summers in the wetlands on the plains. Birds of prey include hawks, eagles, and ospreys, while smaller birds such as robins, orioles, meadowlarks, swallows, and wrens are common. One of the nation's last remaining populations of wild trumpeter swans lives in the Red Rock Lakes National Wildlife Refuge in the southeast corner of the state.

Chapter 2

THE HISTORY OF MONTANA

The first inhabitants of Montana arrived in the region about thirteen thousand years ago. These early settlers were hunters belonging to the Clovis and Folsom cultures. They lived on the plains and in the foothills, moving often to follow the mammoths and other pre-historic mammals they hunted.

About eight thousand years ago, some of this prehistoric population moved into the mountains. They formed communities and lived in small groups, hunting, fishing, and gathering roots, berries, and nuts for food. These groups eventually formed tribes, including the Bannock, Flathead or Salish, and the Kootenai. Around 1600, other Native American tribes from the Great Plains began moving into eastern Montana. These included the Shoshone and the Blackfoot tribes.

Early Exploration

Spanish explorers first ventured into Montana in the 1500s, but the first explorers to record their visit were French brothers Francois and Louis-Joseph de la Vérendrye, who entered the southeastern corner of

OREGON COUNTRY

LOUISIANA

ILLINOIS TERR 1809

MICH TERR 1805

PURCHASE

LOUISIANA TERRITORY 1805

1803

IND TERR (1809)

OHIO 1803

(Spain)

MISSISSIPPI TERR (1804)

ORLEANS TERR 1804

Spain

Lewis and Clark, along with a party including about forty soldiers, interpreters, and guides, traveled up the Missouri River and crossed into Montana in the summer of 1805.

Montana in search of fur in 1743. More explorers, trappers, and traders followed, establishing trading networks with Native American tribes.

France claimed most of the Great Plains region, including Montana, as part of the Louisiana Territory. The lands were ceded to Spain in a 1762 treaty but returned to France in the Treaty of San Ildefonso in 1800. The United States bought the Louisiana Territory from France in 1803 for $15 million. In 1804, President Thomas Jefferson sent a small party led by Meriwether Lewis and William Clark to explore and map the region.

Trappers, Miners, and Bandits

In the wake of the expedition, many fur traders ventured into the state to make their fortune. The American Fur Company established a major trading post along the Missouri River at Fort Union in 1829. Another trading post, called Fort Benton, was established on the Missouri in 1846. However, the fur trade declined sharply in the mid-nineteenth century when fur went out of fashion and the region's beaver population declined.

Gold discoveries in southwest Montana in 1858 and 1862 brought fortune seekers to remote places such as Last Chance Gulch, Alder Gulch, and Grasshopper Creek. Mining camps sprang up at sites where gold was discovered. More than six hundred mining camps were established. Some camps grew into towns so quickly that they were called boomtowns. Last Chance Gulch became Helena, Alder Gulch became Virginia City, and Grasshopper Creek became Bannack. Others remained small, or faded almost as quickly as they sprang up.

The gold rush brought many hard-working, honest people to Montana, but it also attracted criminals who took advantage of a lack of law enforcement in mining towns by robbing or cheating people out of their earnings. Groups of citizens called vigilantes tried to fight lawlessness by tracking down and punishing criminals, sometimes without a trial.

In one famous example of vigilante justice, Sheriff Henry Plummer of Virginia City was accused of secretly leading a gang of thieves called the Innocents, who killed more than one hundred people. In 1863, a group of citizens from Virginia City and Bannack formed a vigilante group and eventually captured, tried, and hanged twenty-one men linked to the gang. Sheriff Plummer was captured and hanged without a trial in 1864.

War with Native Americans

Montana's growth brought settlers into conflict with Native Americans in the region. In 1866, Chief Red Cloud of the Lakota Nation declared war against the United States after he discovered that the U.S. Army was crossing Lakota territory without permission.

Several Great Plains tribes fought a series of battles against the U.S. Army throughout the 1870s as they struggled to hold onto their lands throughout the region. In one of their last efforts, warriors

In a photo dating from the late 1880s or early 1900s, Nez Perce tribesman Duncan McDonald and his wife, Quilsuh, pose on horseback.

from the Sioux and Cheyenne joined with several smaller tribes, such as the Gros Ventres and the Arapaho, to fight against the U.S. Army in 1876. Led by Sioux chiefs Sitting Bull and Crazy Horse, they had a major victory in the Battle of Little Bighorn on June 25, 1876, against Lieutenant Colonel George Armstrong Custer's cavalry force.

The victory was one of the last for the Plains tribes. In 1877, Chief Joseph and the remnants of his Nez Perce tribe of Oregon surrendered after several days of fighting as they fled across Montana. By 1880, most of Montana's Native Americans had been forced onto reservations, where many died from malnutrition and European diseases such as smallpox and measles.

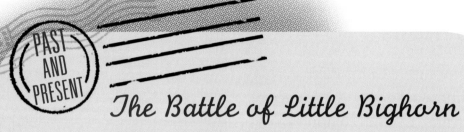

The Battle of Little Bighorn

On June 25, 1876, Lieutenant Colonel George Armstrong Custer led a force of about six hundred men into the valley of the Little Bighorn River in southeastern Montana. Custer and his cavalry force had been sent to the region to fight the Sioux, Lakota, and Cheyenne tribes. As they entered the valley, Custer divided his force into three groups and led one group down into the valley.

As Custer and his men rode into the valley, they met a force of several thousand Sioux and Cheyenne warriors. Custer and his men were surrounded, while his other soldiers were pinned down and unable to reach them. By the end of the battle, Custer and every one of the 209 men he led had been killed. The battle was a great victory for the Native American fighters but came at a high price. The U.S. War Department responded by sending a third of the army to Montana, forcing the remaining members of the Plains tribes onto reservations in just a few short years.

After the battle, Custer was immortalized by the public as a heroic and tragic figure. His "last stand" at Little Bighorn was commemorated in books, paintings, and films. At the battlefield, which became a national monument in 1946, the story of the battle was told almost exclusively from the point of view of the U.S. Cavalry. The Native Americans who actually won the battle were largely ignored. Many descendants of the Native Americans who fought there felt unwelcome at the park.

Today, the park tells a more balanced story. A prominent memorial that commemorates the Native Americans who fought there and offers their interpretations of the battle was dedicated in 2003. Native American descendants also take part in the annual Great Sioux Nation Victory Ride, following the paths of their ancestors to the site on the anniversary of the battle to take part in three days of religious services, academic talks, and celebrations.

Statehood and Growth

Montana's population grew from 39,000 to 143,000 during the 1880s, as settlers came to establish farms and ranches on the plains and to mine for gold, silver, and copper in the mountains. In 1884, the territorial government began pushing for statehood. To become a state, Montana needed a population of at least sixty thousand and a state constitution. A constitutional convention of territorial leaders had written a state constitution in 1866, but the draft was lost on the long journey to the printer in St. Louis.

A second constitution was written in 1884 but was rejected by Congress. Delegates to a constitutional convention held in 1889 completed a third state constitution, and Montana formally became the forty-first state that November.

At the beginning of the twentieth century, railroads, newspapers, and towns began encouraging farmers and others through ads and brochures to settle in the eastern part of the state. Thousands of homesteaders arrived, including many immigrants from European countries. Some participated in the U.S. government's Enlarged Homestead Act of 1909 and received 320 acres (130 ha) for free in exchange for living on and improving the land for three years. By 1910, the number of farms in Montana had doubled.

The End of the Boom

In 1917, the United States entered World War I (1914–1918). More than forty thousand soldiers from Montana fought in the war. Montana farmers prospered during the war, as their crops sold at good prices to meet high demand. Many farmers who made a good

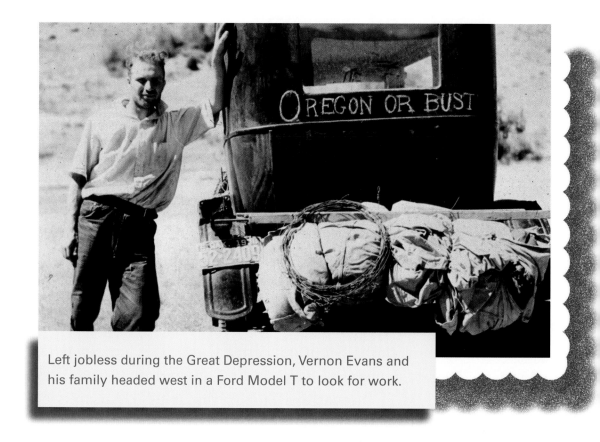

Left jobless during the Great Depression, Vernon Evans and his family headed west in a Ford Model T to look for work.

profit borrowed money to buy more land and new equipment so that they could raise more crops.

By planting so many crops, many farmers exhausted their soil. A drought struck the state in 1918 and persisted until the middle of the 1920s, ruining many farmers. Farmers who had borrowed money had nothing to sell and were unable to repay their debts. About sixty thousand people left the state between 1919 and 1925.

The state suffered during the Great Depression, though New Deal public works programs put some people back to work building new roads, bridges, and dams. Montana prospered again during World

War II (1939–1945), as demand for commodities such as minerals, timber, and the state's agricultural products rose. A large U.S. military base called the Malmstrom Air Force Base near Great Falls was built during the war. It continues to provide many jobs in the region.

An aerial view shows strip mining of Montana coal fields. Montana lies above the nation's largest coal reserves, but it has been decades since a new mine has opened in the state.

Modern Montana

Montana experienced a series of ups and downs through the end of the twentieth century. An energy shortage in the United States during the 1970s helped the state's oil and coal industries. Meanwhile, the state's copper industry lost jobs as the mining process became automated. Farmers and ranchers endured cycles of drought and prosperity. The state's tourism industry suffered a blow in 1988 when forest fires burned through hundreds of thousands of acres of Yellowstone National Park. Huge wildfires also swept the state during a major drought in 2000.

Today, the state's natural beauty, its wide-open space, and the live-and-let-live mentality of its residents continue to attract people to Montana. The state continues to grow, even as it takes on controversial issues, like pollution by its industries and finding new ways to manage its resources.

Chapter 3

THE GOVERNMENT OF MONTANA

As in all U.S. states, Montana is governed at the local, state, and federal levels.

Local governments are found in counties and municipalities. Montana has fifty-six counties. Of those, fifty-three are governed by three county commissioners who are elected to six-year terms, while Ravalli County has five commissioners. In the remaining two—Deer Lodge and Silver Bow—the county government is consolidated with a city government, Anaconda for Deer Lodge and Butte for Silver Bow, and a larger board of commissioners governs with the help of a chief executive. Other elected county officials may include a clerk, treasurer, sheriff, judges, assessor, and coroner. The largest county in Montana is Yellowstone County, where Billings is the county seat.

The State Government

Montana's state government is centered around Helena, which has been the state capital since 1875. Every twenty years, Montana residents vote on whether a constitutional convention should be held and a new state constitution written. In 1972, delegates wrote a new constitution to replace the original document. The 1972 constitution still serves as the basis of government in Montana, guaranteeing residents the right to privacy and the right to live in a clean environment.

The state government of Montana is divided into three branches: the executive, legislative, and judicial. The executive branch, led by the governor, consists of a mix of elected and appointed officials. The governor is the head of the executive branch and serves as commander of the state's police force and militia. In 2008, Democrat Brian Schweitzer was elected to his second term as governor. Other members of the executive branch include the lieutenant governor, secretary of state, attorney general, auditor, and superintendent of public education. These officials are also elected to four-year terms.

Montana's legislature, the governor's office, and various other government agencies are housed in the historic State Capitol, completed in 1902.

The Montana legislature is made up of the house of representatives and the senate and is responsible for making and passing state laws. There are one hundred members of the house of representatives, with each member elected to a two-year term. The senate is made up of fifty members serving four-year terms. Each member represents a different district and is elected by the people living in his or her district. Representatives are limited to serving four terms, and senators cannot serve more than two.

The judicial branch consists of the state's courts. The courts interpret laws passed by the legislature and decide legal cases. There are three levels to Montana's court system. The first level includes city

Minuteman Missiles

At the height of the Cold War against the Soviet Union in the 1960s, the U.S. military developed the Minuteman missiles, which could reach the Soviet Union and were designed to carry nuclear warheads. The missiles were intended to be used to retaliate in the event of a nuclear attack against the United States. They were placed in isolated areas where public land was readily available, far from likely targets.

The first ten Minuteman missiles were placed at Malmstrom Air Force Base near Great Falls in 1962. These were quickly followed by more missile placements on Montana's prairies. By 1970, two hundred of these missiles had been placed in underground silos in central Montana, and many more were located on bases in North and South Dakota, Wyoming, Colorado, Nebraska, and Missouri. The first Minuteman missiles were eventually replaced by the Minuteman II and Minuteman III missile systems, with Malmstrom remaining a major base for the missiles.

The Cold War ended with the fall of the Soviet Union in 1991. In the years that followed, the number of Minuteman missiles was cut in half, and bases in North and South Dakota were eliminated. Today, there are four hundred active Minuteman missiles in the United States. Of those, two hundred remain in Montana.

A 1962 photograph shows a transporter-erector moving a missile into place in its silo at Malmstrom Air Force Base.

and municipal courts, justice of the peace courts, and special courts such as small claims courts and tribal courts. Judges at this level are chosen in local elections. The second level consists of district courts. District courts hear important civil and criminal cases. Montana has fifty-six district courts served by forty-three judges elected to six-year terms. The third level is the supreme court, which reviews rulings of the state's lower courts and decides appeals from the district courts. Six associate justices and one chief justice are elected to eight-year terms on the supreme court.

Tribal Governments

Montana has seven Native American reservations serving as home to eleven tribes. The Flathead Reservation is home to the Flathead, Kootenai, and Pend d'Oreille. The Rocky Boy's Reservation is home to the Chippewa and Cree. Many Assiniboine and the Atsina live at Fort Belknap. Some Assiniboine and the Dakota live at the Fort Peck Reservation. The Blackfoot, Crow, and Northern Cheyenne tribes all live on reservations that are named after them.

Tribal laws govern life on the reservations. Tribal governments run the schools, collect taxes, regulate trade, and maintain relations with federal, state, and local governments. Tribes have their own constitutions, court systems, and police forces. The state cannot collect taxes on reservation land or from transactions that take place on reservations.

National Representatives

Montana sends two senators to the U.S. Senate, where they serve six-year terms. Democrat Max Baucus was reelected to a sixth term in

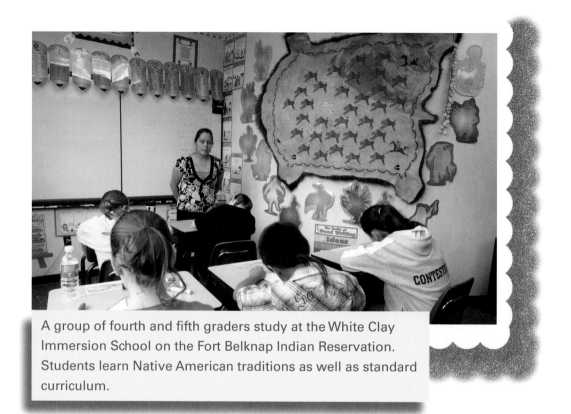

A group of fourth and fifth graders study at the White Clay Immersion School on the Fort Belknap Indian Reservation. Students learn Native American traditions as well as standard curriculum.

2008. Before becoming a senator in 1978, Baucus served in the Montana House of Representatives from 1973 to 1974 and in the U.S. House of Representatives from 1975 to 1978. Democrat Jon Tester was elected to his first term in 2006. Prior to that, he worked as a music teacher and organic farmer and served in the Montana State Senate from 1998 to 2005.

Montana sends only one representative to the U.S. House of Representatives. Montana did have two representatives but lost one after the 1990 U.S. Census showed a population drop. The state, with its more than nine hundred thousand residents, is the largest congressional district by population in the country. In 2008, Republican Denny Rehberg was elected to his fifth term as the state's representative.

Chapter 4

THE ECONOMY OF MONTANA

Montana's economy has undergone many changes since the nineteenth century. The state's first major industry was the fur trade, which prospered until the mid-nineteenth century. Mining for gold, silver, copper, and zinc became the major industry after the gold strikes of the 1850s and 1860s. In the 1880s, ranching and farming became more important, and railroads provided a faster way to ship farm products to markets.

Today, most people in Montana work in service industries, particularly in the wholesale trade of commodities, like agricultural and mineral products, and retail such as grocery stores and gas stations. Other service industry jobs include such personal or community services as work in law firms, doctors' offices, and the insurance, real estate, and finance industries, as well as work for the government ranging from police work and firefighting to assessing taxes. The state's growing tourism industry employs people in hotels and restaurants, as well as at national parks, monuments, and wildlife refuges.

Agriculture and Timber

While severe droughts and extreme weather over the years have taken their toll on the number of farms and ranches on Montana's

A logger prepares to haul away a tree cut for timber. Today, Montana foresters work on sustainable forest management as well as harvesting trees for commercial use.

plains, agriculture remains a significant part of the state's economy, bringing in about $2.9 billion in 2009. Nearly two-thirds of Montana's land is used for agriculture. There are about twenty-two thousand ranches and farms in the state, with each averaging 2,079 acres (841 ha). While Montana ranks second in the nation in ranch and farm acreage, less than 10 percent of its residents make their living through agriculture.

The state's main crop is wheat. Spring wheat is grown in central and northeastern Montana, while winter wheat is grown in the south.

Montana ranks third in the nation in wheat exports. From 2007 to 2008, wheat production increased from 149.8 million bushels to 164.7 million bushels and earned the state about $1.2 billion. Other key crops include barley, corn, oats, rye, sugar beets, seed potatoes, apples, and cherries.

Ranching played a major role in the settlement of eastern Montana during the late nineteenth century, and it continues to have an impact today. Ranchers in the state raise beef cattle, sheep, and hogs. In 2008, there were about 2.6 million head of cattle in Montana, and the cattle industry earned about $1 billion. The state also has a healthy dairy industry, producing milk, cheese, and other products.

Montana has about 22,000,000 acres (9,000,000 ha) of forest. More than 14,000,000 million acres (5.6 million ha) are commercial timberland. The state's timber industry harvests Douglas fir, larch, ponderosa pine, hemlock, Rocky Mountain juniper, red cedar, lodgepole pine, and Engelmann spruce. These trees are used to produce fence posts, plywood, paper, finished lumber, fuel wood, and Christmas trees.

Mining

Montana's mining industry was dominated by gold and silver in the nineteenth century and by copper through much of the twentieth century. The state remains a significant producer of copper, gold, and zinc. In 2007, Montana was the top copper-producing state, with about 750,000 tons (608,000 metric tons) of copper mined. For decades, the state's mining industry was dominated by the powerful Anaconda Company, founded in Butte in 1881. Anaconda closed all of its mining operations in the state in 1983.

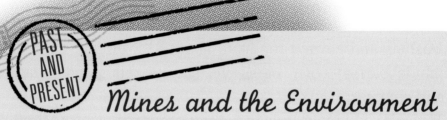

Mines and the Environment

Montana's mineral wealth has been a major part of its economy since the nineteenth century. Resourceful mine operators have used many methods to extract minerals and fossil fuels from the earth. Some of these methods produce harmful chemicals that pollute the environment, like acid runoff that forms from open-pit mines, highly toxic mercury once used to extract gold from lead rocks, and cyanide used today in gold mining. In the past, these chemicals have polluted groundwater in the state and killed plants and wildlife. Former mining sites were often left contaminated and unusable by mining companies.

Today, state laws make it much more difficult for mining companies to leave a site contaminated. The state has banned the use of cyanide in gold mining, and companies are required by the state constitution to clean up their waste through reclamation. Mining operations have to create a plan for reclaiming a site before they are allowed to begin work. When they have finished with their work, they have to restore the landscape. Coal miners, for example, have to rebuild the land after they have removed all of the coal. Gold miners have to collect the cyanide they used and dispose of it.

However, the process of reclaiming old mines poses its own set of problems. For some large open-pit mines, refilling the holes can create environmental hazards. For example, refilling pits in wet areas made up of certain types of rock can cause the release of pollutants such as acids, arsenic, and mercury.

Modern mining operations are doing a better job of cleaning up their waste and refilling open-pit mines and planting them with trees and grasses. Montana has even created a state agency called the Mine Waste Cleanup Bureau that works to reclaim old abandoned mines. However, the agency's task remains huge, as there are more than 3,800 abandoned mines in the state.

Other resources that are mined in Montana include lead, phosphate, gypsum, limestone, gravel, sand, and vermiculite. Montana ranks first in the United States in the production of talc, and 80 percent of known chrome reserves in North America are located in the state. Montana is also a leading producer of gem-stones, including sapphires, agates, and garnets.

A miner takes a break while working 3,250 feet (990 meters) below ground in a mine near Nye, Montana.

Coal, oil, and natural gas are the most important minerals extracted in Montana, accounting for about 80 percent of the state's income from mining. Soft subbituminous coal is found throughout southeastern Montana. The coal is removed from the ground using strip-mining techniques that take away layers of soil and rock to get to the minerals underneath. Machines do much of the work, so while mining provides a significant portion of Montana's income, it is no longer a major source of employment.

Petroleum and natural gas production is a growing industry in Montana. Oil production began in Montana in the 1920s and is focused in the Elk Basin, Bell Creek, Williston Basin, and Cut Bank oil fields, while most of the state's natural gas comes from the

A farmer watches an oil derrick pump drill for oil in a field. Exploiting reserves in northeastern Montana could someday dramatically increase the state's oil production.

Williston Basin. The state produces about 1 percent of the nation's petroleum but could produce more in the years to come. A geological survey completed in 2008 found that a massive shale formation located in eastern Montana and western North Dakota could hold between 3 and 4.3 billion barrels of oil.

Manufacturing

Long overshadowed by mining and farming, manufacturing remains a small part of Montana's economy. Manufacturing employs about 6 percent of the state's workers and consists mainly of processing raw materials. Sawmills turn western Montana's timber into wood products that eventually become items such as prefabricated homes, telephone poles, plywood, and pencils. Major oil refineries are located in Billings, Laurel, Cut Bank, and Great Falls, and the world's leading lead smelter is in East Helena. Printing, paper manufacturing, and concrete production are all industries in Montana.

Food processing in the state is concentrated in Great Falls and Billings. Major food-processing operations include plants that pack meat, process milk, mill grain, and bottle soft drinks. The push for more sources of renewable energy has led to the construction of wind farms and biodiesel plants in Montana.

Chapter 5

PEOPLE FROM MONTANA:
PAST AND PRESENT

Although a small state by population, Montana has produced its share of illustrious figures, ranging from scientists and businessmen to actors and professional daredevils.

Plenty Coups (1848–1932) Crow chief Plenty Coups was a fierce warrior and skilled diplomat who led his people away from hunting and gathering to a more agricultural way of life. He worked hard to negotiate peace with the U.S. government and to preserve the culture and traditions of his people. He was named chief of all the Crow in 1904.

Marcus Daly (1841–1900) In 1876, mining speculator Marcus Daly bought the Anaconda silver mine in Butte. The mine turned out to contain vast deposits of copper and made Daly one of the richest and most powerful men in Montana. He founded the town of Anaconda, and his Anaconda Mining Company eventually branched out into timber, banking, and coal mining.

John R. Horner (1946–) John Horner is one of the best-known paleontologists in the United States. His discoveries

Paleontologist John Horner discusses his 2009 book, *How to Build a Dinosaur: Extinction Doesn't Have to Be Forever*, at the Museum of the Rockies, Bozeman, where he is curator.

include the first dinosaur eggs found in the Western Hemisphere and have led to new theories on how dinosaurs behaved. He is the author of several books and hundreds of articles on dinosaurs, and he worked as technical adviser on the *Jurassic Park* films.

Dorothy Johnson (1905–1984) Dorothy Johnson was a journalist and Western novelist. Her works include *The Man Who Shot Liberty Valance* and *A Man Called Horse*, which were made into successful movies. Johnson also taught at Montana State University.

Evel Knievel (1938–2007) Motorcycle daredevil Evel Knievel was once fired as a teenager from a mining job for

Actors from Montana

Since the early days of film, some of Hollywood's biggest stars have come from Montana. Actress Myrna Loy (1905–1993) was born in Radersburg and appeared in many silent films before becoming famous for playing Nora Charles in *The Thin Man* and its several sequels. Martha Raye (1916–1994) began her career as a singer and actress on the vaudeville stage before shifting to comic roles in films in the 1930s and 1940s and later to television.

George Montgomery (1916–2000) played in dozens of Westerns during a career that spanned six decades and eighty-seven films, often playing secondary characters before landing several leading roles in the early 1940s. Gary Cooper (1901–1961) began acting in silent films and went on to become one of Hollywood's most recognizable stars. He earned an Academy Award for Best Actor in 1941 for *Sergeant York* and again in 1952 for *High Noon*.

Later stars have also had a major impact in Hollywood. Peter Fonda (1940–) rose to prominence as an actor during the 1960s and is best known for his role as a biker in the iconic film *Easy Rider*. Dana Carvey (1955–) first became famous for his work on the television sketch-comedy show *Saturday Night Live* and had a major film hit with *Wayne's World*. Michelle Williams (1980–) starred in the hit television drama *Dawson's Creek* before moving on to roles in acclaimed independent films such as *The Station Agent* and earning several awards and nominations for her role in *Brokeback Mountain*.

Myrna Loy made her stage debut at a Helena theater at age twelve. She received an Academy Award for Lifetime Achievement in 1991.

downing a major power line by popping a wheelie with an earthmover. Knievel jumped mountain lions, Las Vegas fountains, buses, and much more, breaking dozens of bones throughout his lifetime.

David Lynch (1946–) Born in Missoula, director David Lynch is known for movies that have bizarre, dream-like elements. His works include *Eraserhead*, *The Elephant Man*, *Blue Velvet*, *Mulholland Drive*, and the television series *Twin Peaks*. Lynch was twice nominated for the Academy Award for Best Director.

Mike Mansfield (1903–2001) Mike Mansfield served in the U.S. House of Representatives from 1942 to 1953 and in the U.S. Senate from 1953 to 1977. He was Democratic Majority Leader in the Senate from 1961 to 1977. The powerful and influential Mansfield coauthored the Twenty-Sixth Amendment to the U.S. Constitution, which lowered the legal voting age from twenty-one to eighteen.

Colin Meloy (1974–) Helena native Colin Meloy is a founding member and the lead singer of the acclaimed folk-rock band the Decemberists. The group approaches songs as storytelling and draws heavily on literary themes. Their ambitious albums include *The Crane Wife* and *The Hazards of Love*.

Charley Pride (1938–) Before becoming a major country music star, singer Charley Pride worked as a tin smelter in Helena. He went on to record twenty-nine number-one hit singles and win seven Grammy Awards. In 2000, he became the first African American inducted into the Country Music Hall of Fame.

Charles Marion Russell (1864–1926) Western artist Charles Marion Russell worked as a cowboy and painted and sculpted in his spare time before making his first major sales in Lewiston in 1891. His work depicted the lives of cowboys, Native Americans, and outlaws, and his pictures were printed in numerous magazines. His mural *Lewis and Clark Meeting the Flathead Indians* is in the Montana State Capitol.

Charley Pride rose to stardom with such hits as "Kiss an Angel Good Morning." He was also a baseball player who at one point played for the East Helena Smelterites.

Ted Turner (1938–) Businessman and philanthropist Ted Turner is the founder of several innovative cable television networks, including the Cable News Network (CNN) and Turner Classic Movies. Turner's gift of $1 billion launched the United Nations Foundation, a charity that funds UN projects. His main home is a ranch outside Bozeman, where he raises bison.

Timeline

12,000–9,000 BCE	Clovis and Folsom cultures settle in Montana, followed by other Native American groups.
1743	Montana is first visited by French explorers.
1762	Spain takes possession of Montana from France.
1803	The United States acquires most of Montana from France in the Louisiana Purchase.
1805–1806	Lewis and Clark explore Montana.
1846	Fort Benton becomes the first permanent European settlement in Montana.
1858–1862	The Montana gold rush begins.
1864	The Montana Territory is created.
1876	Native Americans defeat George Custer at the Battle of Little Bighorn.
1877	Chief Joseph and the Nez Perce tribe surrender in Montana.
1881	The Anaconda Mining Company is founded.
1889	Montana becomes the forty-first state.
1910	The U.S. government creates Glacier National Park.
1916	Jeannette Rankin becomes the first woman elected to the U.S. House of Representatives.
1918–1925	Montana loses population due to a severe drought.
1946	The site of the Battle of Little Bighorn becomes a national monument.
1962	The first Minuteman missiles are placed on Montana's prairie.
1972	Montana delegates write a new state constitution.
1988	Wildfires devastate Yellowstone National Park.
1996	The FBI captures members of the Freemen militia group after an eighty-one-day standoff. Unabomber Theodore Kaczynski is captured.
2008	Governor Brian Schweitzer is elected to a second term in office.

State motto:	*Oro y Plata* ("Gold and Silver")
State capital:	Helena
State flower:	Bitterroot
State bird:	Western meadowlark
State tree:	Ponderosa pine
State song:	"Montana"
Statehood date and number:	November 9, 1889; forty-first state
State nicknames:	The Treasure State, Big Sky Country
Total area and U.S. rank:	147,046 square miles (380,847 sq km); fourth-largest state
Population:	967,440
Highest elevation:	Humphrey's Peak, at 12,799 feet (3,901 m)
Lowest elevation:	Kootenai River, at 1,800 feet (549 m)

State Flag

State Seal

Major rivers:	Missouri River, Yellowstone River, Gallatin River, Jefferson River, Madison River, Sun River, Teton River, Milk River, Bighorn River
Major lakes:	Flathead Lake, Fort Peck Lake, Lonesome Lake, Benton Lake, Red Rock Lake
Hottest recorded temperature:	117°F (47°C) at Medicine Lake on July 5, 1937, and at Glendive on July 20, 1893
Coldest recorded temperature:	-70°F (-57°C) at Rogers Pass on January 20, 1954
Origin of state name:	Taken from the Spanish word for "mountainous"
Chief agricultural products:	Cattle, hogs, sheep, wheat, barley, sugar beets, cherries
Major industries:	Mining, fossil fuels, timber, paper products and printing, wood products

Western meadowlark

Bitterroot

canyon A long, deep, narrow valley with steep cliff walls, often formed by running water and having a river or stream at the bottom.

constitution The system of fundamental laws and principles that prescribes the nature, functions, and limits of a government or other institution.

drought A long period of abnormally low rainfall, especially one that adversely affects growing or living conditions.

ecosystem A system formed by a community of organisms and their interactions with their physical environment.

geyser A natural hot spring that intermittently discharges jets of water and steam into the air.

glacier A huge mass of ice formed over a long period of time that moves slowly across a landmass and does not melt in the summer.

homesteader A settler who works a piece of land in order to acquire title to the property.

mineral A substance, such as stone, coal, or sand, that is obtained by mining.

plateau An area of relatively flat, elevated ground.

prairie An area of flat, treeless grassland.

precipitation Any form of water that falls to the earth's surface, such as rain or snow.

reservation A federally owned tract of land managed by a Native American tribe.

sagebrush A small aromatic shrub with silver-green wedge-shaped leaves and clusters of yellow flowers that grows in semiarid regions of the American West.

smelt To refine metals by heating.

tectonic plate A large segment of the earth's crust that moves relative to other plates.

tundra A northern treeless plain where the subsoil is permanently frozen.

Glacier National Park

P.O. Box 128

West Glacier, MT 59936

(406) 888-7800

Web site: http://www.nps.gov/glac

Visitors can find information about Glacier National Park through the National Park Service Web site.

Little Bighorn Battlefield National Monument

P.O. Box 39

Crow Agency, MT 59022

(406) 638-2621

Web site: http://www.nps.gov/libi

Visitors can find information about the Little Bighorn Battlefield National Monument through the National Park Service Web site.

Montana Historical Society

P.O. Box 201201

225 North Roberts

Helena, MT 59620-1201

(406) 444-2694

Web site: http://www.his.state.mt.us

This agency, founded in 1865, is devoted to Montana history.

Montana Official State Travel Site

(800) 847-4868

http://www.visitmt.com

Visitors can access information about vacation, recreation, and accommodations in Montana.

Montana's Official State Web Site

http://www.mt.gov

Montana's official Web site provides access to information about the state's government.

Yellowstone National Park

P.O. Box 168

Yellowstone National Park, WY 82190-0168

(307) 344-7381

http://www.nps.gov/yell

The National Park Service site for Yellowstone National Park provides visitors with information about the park and tools for trip planning.

Web Sites

Due to the changing nature of Internet links, Rosen Publishing has developed an online list of Web sites related to the subject of this book. This site is updated regularly. Please use this link to access the list:

http://www.rosenlinks.com/uspp/mtpp

Aretha, David. *Glacier National Park: Adventure, Explore, Discover*. Berkeley Heights, NJ: Enslow Publishing, 2009.

Brust, James S., et al. *Where Custer Fell: Photographs of the Little Bighorn Battlefield Then and Now*. Norman, OK: University of Oklahoma Press, 2007.

Bryant, Annie. *Ghost Town*. Lexington, MA: B*tween Productions, 2007.

Harmon, Michael B. *The Last Exit to Normal*. New York, NY: Alfred A. Knopf, 2008.

Heinrichs, Ann. *Montana*. Minneapolis, MN: Compass Point Books, 2004.

Holmes, Krys. *Montana: Stories of the Land*. Helena, MT: Montana Historical Society Press, 2009.

Ingold, Jeanette. *Hitch*. Orlando, FL: Harcourt, Inc., 2005.

Larson, Kirby. *Hattie Big Sky*. New York, NY: Delacorte Press, 2006.

Lemna, Don. *When the Sergeant Came Marching Home*. New York, NY: Holiday House, 2008.

Marrin, Albert. *Years of Dust*. New York, NY: Dutton Children's Books, 2009.

Rand, Johnathan. *Mutant Mammoths of Montana*. Topinabee Island, MI: AudioCraft, 2007.

Spencer, Janet. *Montana Trivia*. Helena, MT: Riverbend Publishing, 2005.

Thomas, Jane Resh. *Blind Mountain*. New York, NY: Clarion Books, 2006.

Vasapoli, Salvatore. *Montana: Portrait of a State*. Portland, OR: Graphic Arts Center Publishing Company, 2008.

Wolf, Allan. *New Found Land: Lewis and Clark's Voyage of Discovery*. Cambridge, MA: Candlewick Press, 2007.

BIBLIOGRAPHY

Crown of the Continent. "About the Crown of the Continent." Retrieved November 22, 2009 (http://www.crownofthecontinent.net/about.php).

Dunn, Jerry Camarillo. *The Smithsonian Guide to Historic America: Rocky Mountain States*. New York, NY: Stewart, Tabori & Chang, 1989.

Haynes, George. "Outlook for Montana Agriculture." *Montana Business Quarterly*, March 22, 2009. Retrieved November 22, 2009 (http://www.thefreelibrary.com/Outlook + for + Montana + agriculture.-a0198932768).

Howard, Joseph Kinsey. *Montana: High, Wide, and Handsome*. Lincoln, NE: University of Nebraska Press, 2003.

Hutchison, Sayre. "History of Minuteman Missile Sites." National Park Service, November 13, 2009. Retrieved November 22, 2009 (http://www.nps.gov/archive/mimi/history/srs/intro.htm).

LaForge, John. "Missile Fields Still Armed and Dangerous." *Nukewatch Quarterly*, Winter 2006–07. Retrieved November 22, 2009 (http://www.nukewatch.com/weapons/index.html).

McCoy, Michael. *Montana Off the Beaten Path: A Guide to Unique Places*. Old Saybrook, CT: Globe Pequot Press, 1993.

McRae, W. C., and Judy Jewell. *Montana*. 6th ed. Emeryville, CA: Avalon Travel Publishing, 2005.

Minard, Anne. "No More Glaciers in Glacier National Park by 2020?" *National Geographic News*, March 2, 2009. Retrieved November 22, 2009 (http://news.national geographic.com/news/2009/03/090302-glaciers-melting.html).

Oliver, Myrna. "Cowboy Actor, Entertainer George Montgomery Dies." *Los Angeles Times*, December 14, 2000. Retrieved November 22, 2009 (http://www.amarillo.com/stories/121400/usn_montgomery.shtml).

Perrottet, Tony. "Little Bighorn Reborn." *Smithsonian*, April 2005. Retrieved November 22, 2009 (http://www.smithsonianmag.com/travel/des_bighorn.html).

USDA Economic Research Service. "State Fact Sheet: Montana." October 21, 2009. Retrieved November 22, 2009 (http://www.ers.usda.gov/StateFacts/mt.htm).

U.S. Geological Survey. "3 to 4.3 Billion Barrels of Technically Recoverable Oil Assessed in North Dakota and Montana's Bakken Formation." April 10, 2008. Retrieved November 22, 2009 (http://www.usgs.gov/newsroom/article.asp?ID = 1911).

Tirrell, Norma. *Montana*. 6th ed. New York, NY: Compass American Guides, 2006.

Tuttle, Steve. "R.I.P., Evel Knievel." *Newsweek*, November 30, 2007. Retrieved November 22, 2009 (http://www.newsweek.com/id/73206).

INDEX

About the Author

Jason Porterfield is a journalist and writer living in Chicago, Illinois. He graduated from Oberlin College, where he majored in English, history, and religion. In 2008, he earned an M.A. in journalism from Columbia College, Chicago. He has written more than twenty books for Rosen Publishing, including one on his home state of Virginia.

Photo Credits

Cover (top left), p. 15 MPI/Hulton Archive/Getty Images; cover (top right), p. 31 Bloomberg via Getty Images; cover (bottom), pp. 3, 6, 8, 9, 14, 22, 23, 27, 34, 39, 41 Shutterstock.com; p. 4 © GeoAtlas; p. 7 John Wang/The Image Bank/Getty Images; p. 13 NPS Photo by Jim Peaco; p. 17 Transcendental Graphics/Hulton Archive/Getty Images; p. 20 Arthur Rothstein/Hulton Archive/Getty Images; p. 21 Emory Kristof/National Geographic/Getty Images; p. 24 James P. Blair/National Geographic/Getty Images; pp. 26, 35 © AP Images; p. 28 © www.istockphoto.com/Bob Hosea; p. 32 Chris Cheadle/Riser/Getty Images; p. 36 Popperfoto/Getty Images; p. 38 Mike Prior/Redferns/Getty Images; p. 40 (left) Courtesy of Robesus, Inc.

Designer: Les Kanturek; Editor: Karolena Bielecki
    Photo Researcher: Peter Tomlinson